MAPS

Pebble®

T0084930

# Symbols and Keys

by
Jennifer M. Besel

Consulting editor:
Gail Saunders-Smith, PhD

Consultant:
Dr. Sarah E. Battersby
Department of Geography
University of South Carolina

CAPSTONE PRESS
a capstone imprint

Pebble Books are published by Capstone Press,
1710 Roe Crest Drive, North Mankato, Minnesota 56003
www.capstonepub.com

Copyright © 2014 by Capstone Press, a Capstone imprint. All rights reserved.
No part of this publication may be reproduced in whole or in part, or stored in a retrieval system, or transmitted in any form or by any means, electronic, mechanical, photocopying, recording, or otherwise, without written permission of the publisher.

**Library of Congress Cataloging-in-Publication Data**
Besel, Jennifer M.
Symbols and keys / by Jennifer M. Besel.
pages. cm.—(Pebble Books. Maps)
Includes bibliographical references and index.
Summary: "Simple text with full-color photos and illustrations provide basic information about map symbols and keys"—Provided by publisher.
ISBN 978-1-4765-3082-6 (library binding)—ISBN 978-1-4765-3504-3 (ebook pdf)—ISBN 978-1-4765-3522-7 (paperback)
1. Maps—Symbols—Juvenile literature. 2. Map scales—Juvenile literature. I. Title.
GA155B47 2014
912.01'48—dc23 2012046452

**Editorial Credits**
Gene Bentdahl, designer; Kathy McColley, production specialist; Sarah Schuette, photo stylist; Marcy Morin, scheduler

**Photo Credits**
Capstone: 7, 9, 11, 13, 15 (top), 17, 19, 21; Capstone Studio: Karon Dubke, cover, 1, 5, 15 (bottom)

# Note to Parents and Teachers

The Maps set supports social studies standards related to people, places, and environments. This book describes and illustrates map symbols and keys. The images support early readers in understanding the text. The repetition of words and phrases helps early readers learn new words. This book also introduces early readers to subject-specific vocabulary words, which are defined in the Glossary section. Early readers may need assistance to read some words and to use the Table

Printed in the United States 5038

MAPS

# Table of Contents


Shapes on a Map . . . . . 4
Shape Symbols . . . . . 10
Picture Symbols . . . . . 16
Color Symbols . . . . . 20

Glossary . . . . . 22
Read More . . . . . 23
Internet Sites. . . . . 23
Critical Thinking Using the Common Core. . . 24
Index . . . . . 24

# Shapes on a Map

Maps have funny shapes
all over them. What are
those shapes?
They're map symbols,
and they are helpful map tools.

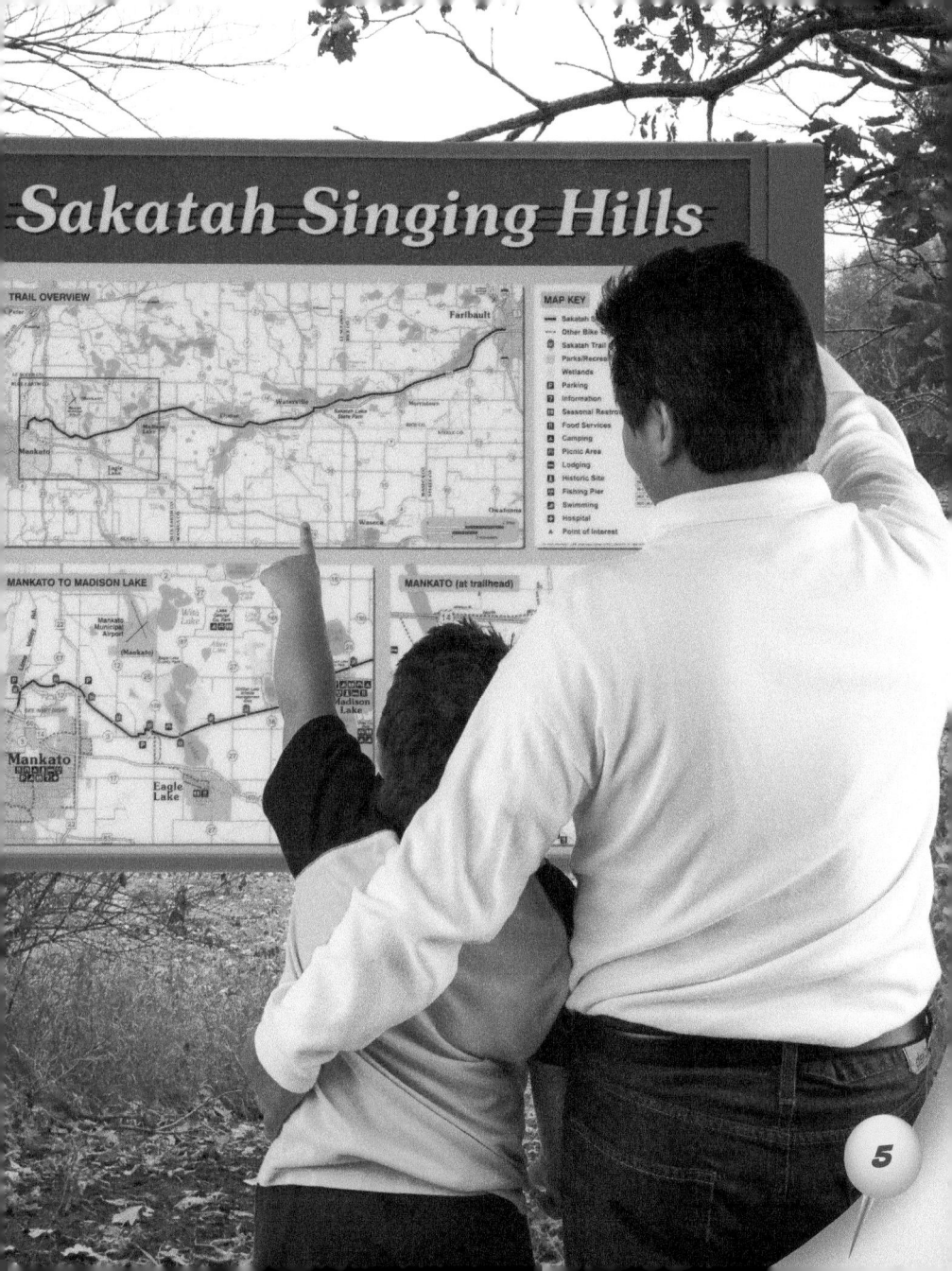
Sakatah Singing Hills
TRAIL OVERVIEW
Fairbault
Waterville
Mankato
Owatonna
Waseca
MAP KEY
Parking
Information
Food Services
Camping
Picnic Area
Lodging
Historic Site
Fishing Pier
Swimming
Hospital
Point of Interest
MANKATO TO MADISON LAKE
Mankato Municipal Airport
(Mankato)
Mankato
Eagle Lake
MANKATO (at trailhead)

Maps show places on Earth.
But to make the places fit
on a small map,
mapmakers use symbols.
Symbols are shapes
that stand for real things.

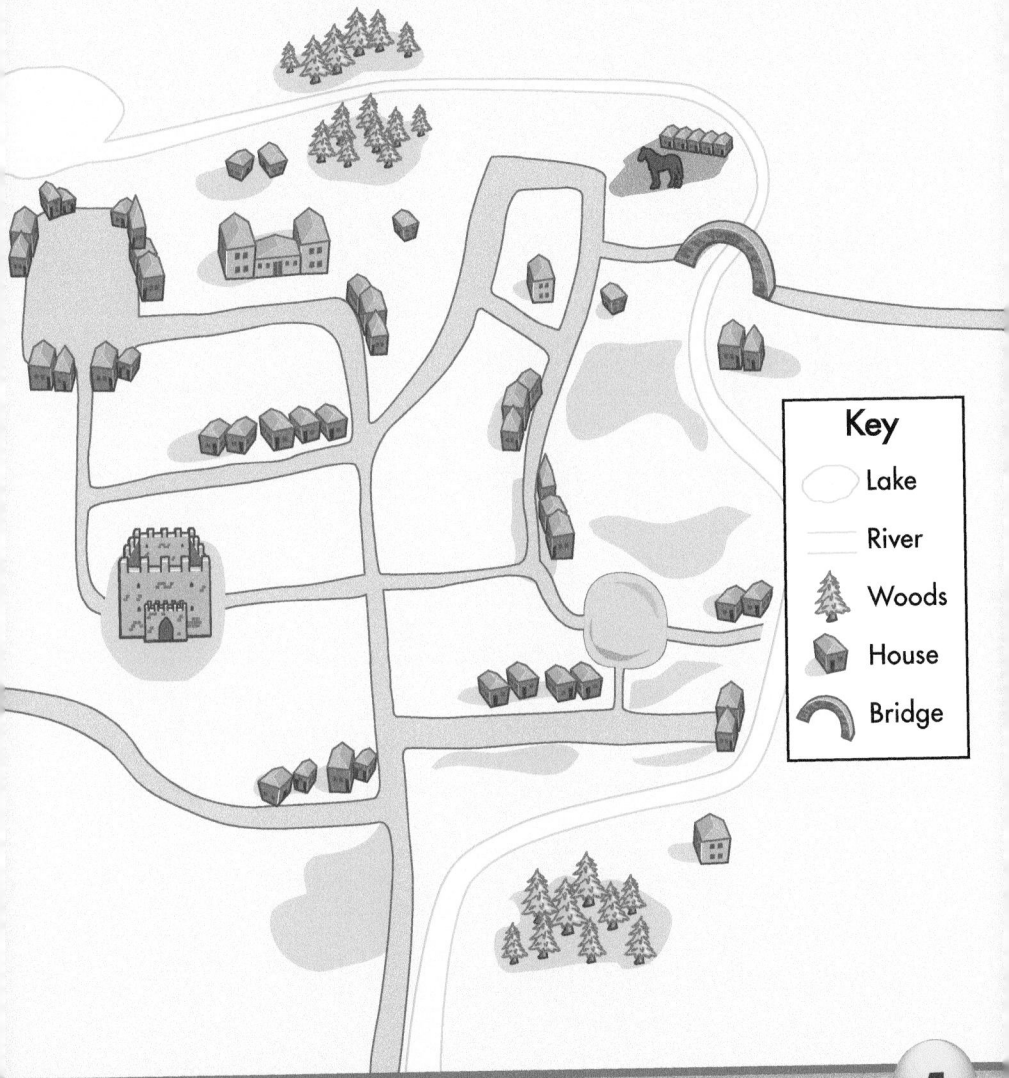
Key
Lake
River
Woods
House
Bridge

Each map has a chart
that tells what
the symbols mean.
This chart is called
a key or legend.

# Key

Bike path

Post office

Library

Hospital

Fire station

Police station

School

Town hall

Downtown

Parking

# Shape Symbols

Some maps use shape symbols.

A circle might be a town.

A square could be a building.

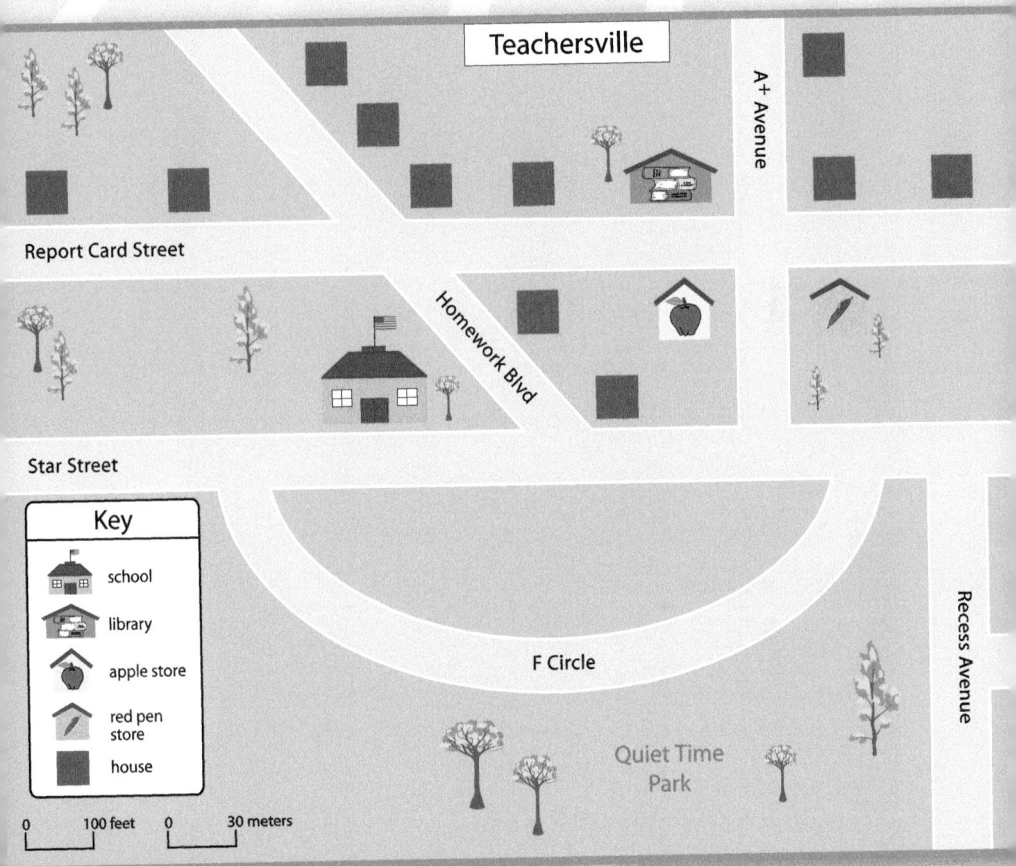
Teachersville
A+ Avenue
Report Card Street
Homework Blvd
Star Street
Key
school
library
apple store
red pen store
house
F Circle
Recess Avenue
Quiet Time Park
0 100 feet
0 30 meters

Road maps use black dots
to stand for cities.
Colored lines are roads.

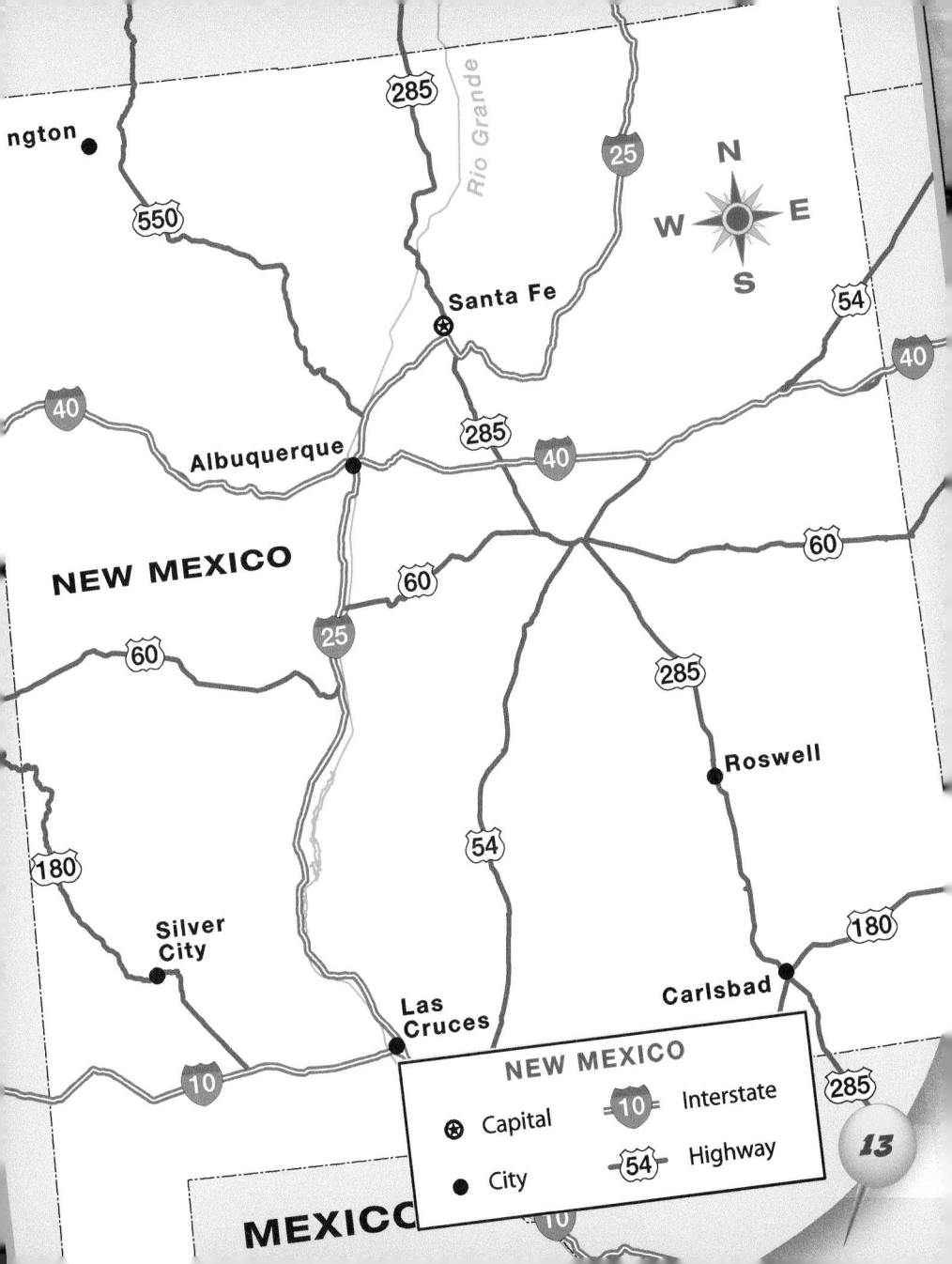
ngton
285
Rio Grande
25
550
N
W
E
S
Santa Fe
54
40
40
285
Albuquerque
40
NEW MEXICO
60
60
25
60
285
Roswell
54
180
Silver City
180
Carlsbad
Las Cruces
10
285
NEW MEXICO
Capital
City
10
Interstate
54
Highway
MEXICO
10

Maps of buildings
use shape symbols too.
Symbols show where
to find stairs or exits.

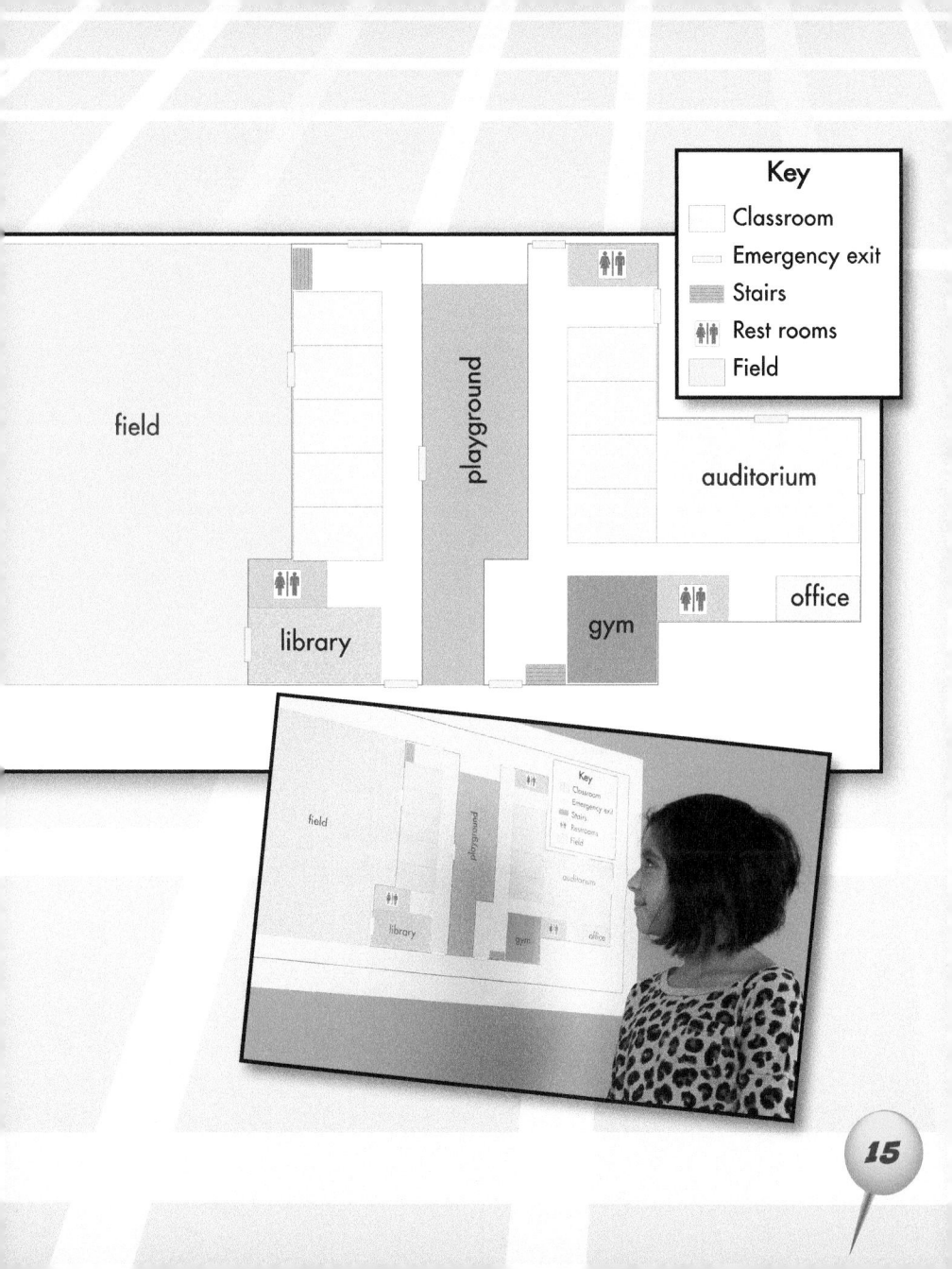
Key
Classroom
Emergency exit
Stairs
Rest rooms
Field
field
playground
auditorium
library
gym
office

# Picture Symbols

Some maps use symbols
that look like
the things they stand for.
A sun stands for a sunny day
on a weather map.

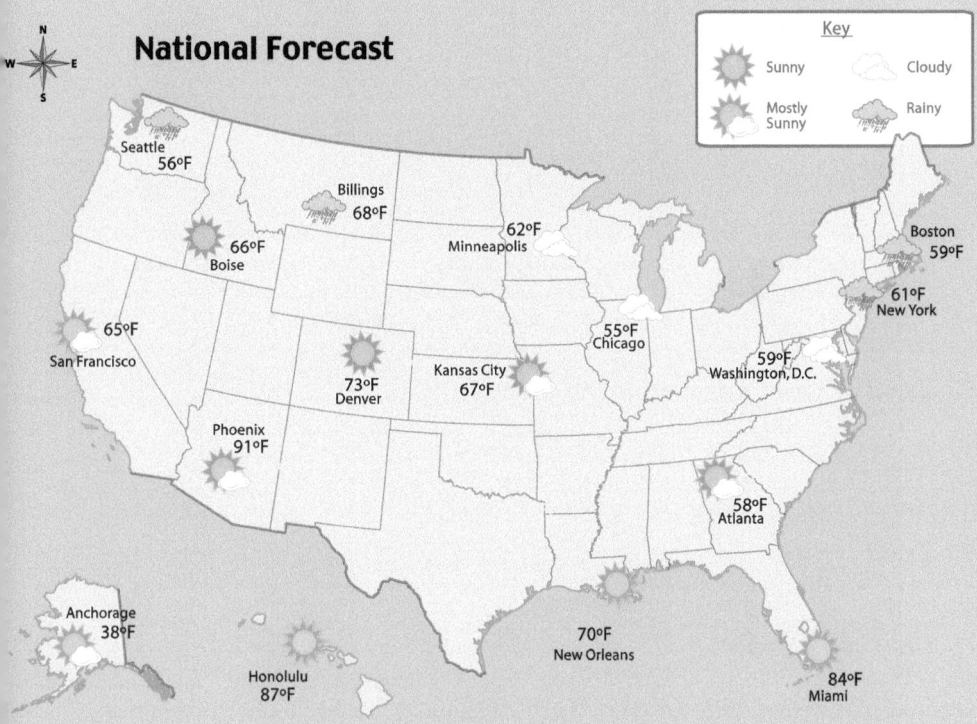
National Forecast
N
W
E
S
Key
Sunny
Cloudy
Mostly Sunny
Rainy
Seattle
56ºF
Billings
68ºF
66ºF
Boise
62ºF
Minneapolis
Boston
59ºF
61ºF
New York
65ºF
San Francisco
55ºF
Chicago
73ºF
Denver
Kansas City
67ºF
59ºF
Washington, D.C.
Phoenix
91ºF
58ºF
Atlanta
Anchorage
38ºF
70ºF
New Orleans
Honolulu
87ºF
84ºF
Miami

Some maps even use
pictures as symbols.
A picture of a bear
on a zoo map
shows where the bears live.

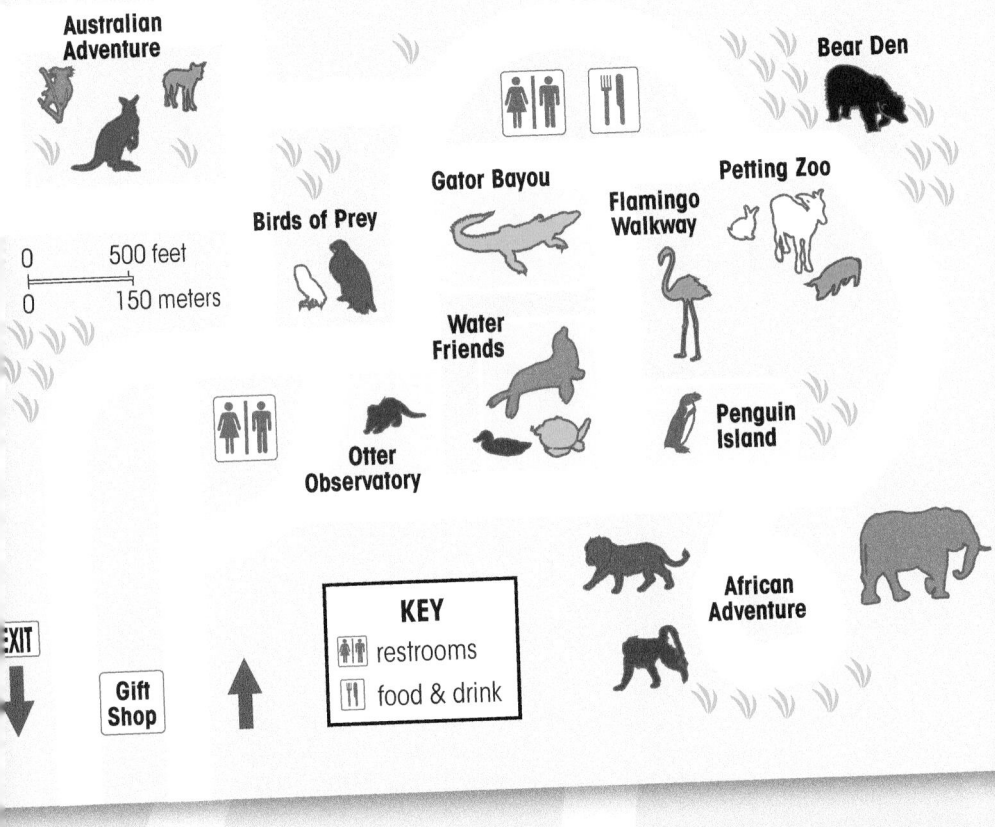
Australian Adventure
Bear Den
Gator Bayou
Petting Zoo
Flamingo Walkway
Birds of Prey
0 500 feet
0 150 meters
Water Friends
Penguin Island
Otter Observatory
African Adventure
KEY
restrooms
food & drink
EXIT
Gift Shop

# Color Symbols

Colors can be symbols too.

Red can stand for hot weather.

Symbols really are a colorful,

helpful map tool.

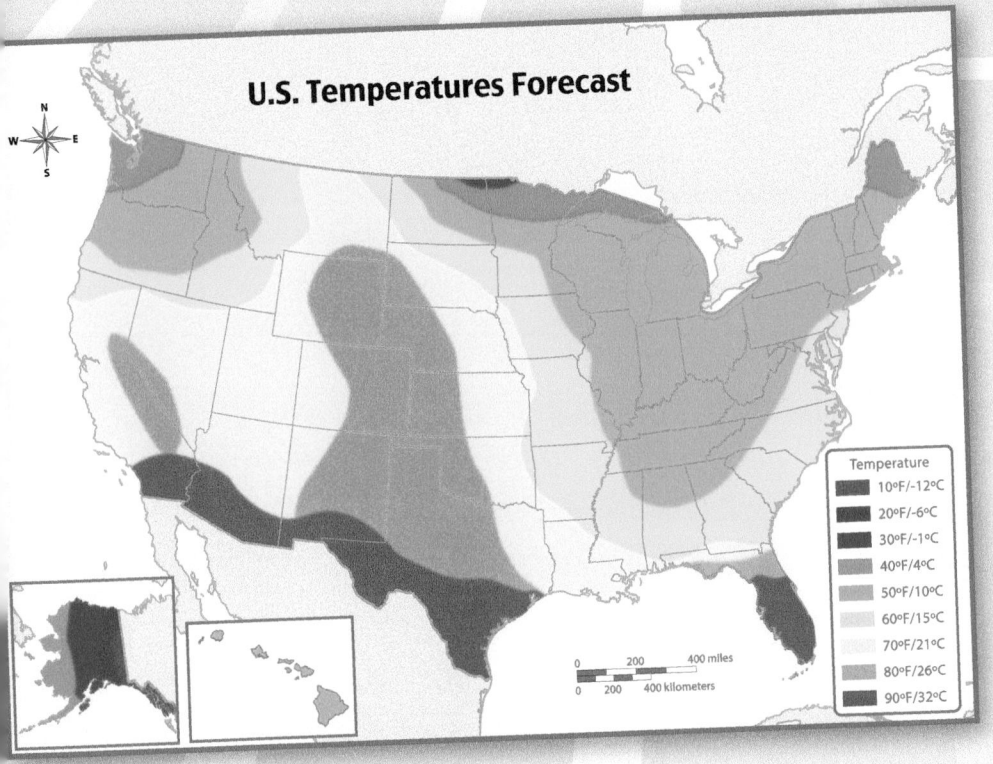
U.S. Temperatures Forecast
N
W
E
S
Temperature
10ºF/-12ºC
20ºF/-6ºC
30ºF/-1ºC
40ºF/4ºC
50ºF/10ºC
60ºF/15ºC
70ºF/21ºC
80ºF/26ºC
90ºF/32ºC
0 200 400 miles
0 200 400 kilometers

# Glossary

**chart**—something that shows information in the form of a picture or graph

**key**—a list or chart that explains symbols on a map or graph

**legend**—a chart that explains symbols on a map; legend is another name for a map key

**symbol**—an object that stands for something else

**weather**—the condition outdoors at a certain time and place; weather changes with each season

# Read More

**Besel, Jennifer M.** *Types of Maps.* Maps. North Mankato, Minn.: Capstone Press, 2014.

**Greve, Meg**. *Keys and Symbols on Maps.* Little World Geography. Vero Beach, Fla.: Rourke Pub., 2010.

**Spilsbury, Louise**. *Mapping.* Investigate. Chicago: Heinemann Library, 2010.

# Internet Sites

FactHound offers a safe, fun way to find Internet sites related to this book. All of the sites on FactHound have been researched by our staff.

Here's all you do:

Visit *www.facthound.com*

Type in this code: 9781476530826

Check out projects, games and lots more at
**www.capstonekids.com**

# Critical Thinking Using the Common Core

1. Describe the steps to use a key to find a location on a map. (Key Ideas and Details)
2. Look at the maps on pages 13 and 19. What are some of the major differences and similarities between maps that use shape symbols and maps that use picture symbols? (Craft and Structure)
3. Look at the maps on pages 17 and 21. Both maps show information related to weather. Describe the differences between these maps. When would each of these maps be most useful? (Integration of Knowledge and Ideas)

# Index


buildings, 10, 14

cities, 12
color symbols, 20

Earth, 6

keys, 8

legends, 8

picture symbols, 16, 18

roads, 12

shape symbols, 10, 12, 14

towns, 10

weather, 16, 20

zoo, 18



Word Count: 173
Grade: 1
Early-Intervention Level: 16